Praise for Deep Learning Manual

"Every now and then you run into a book that transforms your fundamental thinking. Not only is this book fun to read, it will reset your learning process. This is one of those rare books that I will carry around with me. This book is to be read and studied, re-read and re-studied, and incorporated into our fundamental outlook and learning process."

> Tom McCabe, Founder, McCabe Software
> and Expanded Consciousness Institute

"The Deep Learning Manual makes new insights deceptively easy. Short chapters take you through lively lessons, and without realizing it, you've found new ways to use your mind. Art Murray has given us a guide to go beyond rote knowledge into the depths of understanding."

> Dr. William E. Halal, Professor Emeritus,
> The George Washington University;
> Founder and Chairman, TechCast™ Global

"Dr. Murray offers a common sense guide to a style of teaching that has its foundations in the Classical Age. The principles outlined in this manual are both tried and true and revolutionary, dependent upon one's perspective. In either case, parents and concerned educators should demand the consideration of its principles, which have been tested, tried and have proven to produce genuine learning, laced with understanding and wisdom!"

> Dr. Fred Snowden, Founder,
> Virginia Academy; faculty, The OVO School,
> Guangdong Province, China

"How do you prefer to learn? Murray's Deep Learning Manual is indeed a knowledge explorer's guide to self-discovery. And while it begins posing two points of view, as it provides exercises for expanding your powers of observation and writing to learn, it becomes quite clear that learning is in the hands of the learner. So sharpen your #2 pencil, climb on board that beam of light, and embrace the deep learning cycle. Your life may never be the same."

> Drs. Alex and David Bennet, Co-Founders,
> Mountain Quest Institute

"A compelling Primer that draws all the way from pencil and paper to quantum in describing a new approach for stimulating out-of-the-box thinking, superior learning, and personal discovery."

> Dr. Dan Holtshouse, former Director,
> Corporate Strategy, Xerox Corporation

"Just as business and education are realizing the need to move from a 'shallow' learning approach of memorizing facts, this breakthrough book provides the basics - and blueprint - for how to approach 'deep' learning."

> Dr. John Lewis, Co-Founder,
> The CoHero Institute for Collaborative
> Leadership in Learning Organizations

Deep Learning Manual

The knowledge explorer's guide to self-discovery in education, work, and life

Arthur J. Murray

Copyright © 2016 by Arthur J. Murray
All rights reserved. No part of this publication may be reproduced, distributed, or transmitted in any form or by any means, or stored in a database or retrieval system, without the prior written permission of the copyright owner.

ISBN-10: 0692553797
ISBN-13: 978-0692553794

Published by: Applied Knowledge Sciences Press
Printed in the United States of America

Contents

Manifesto iii

Preface v

Introduction 1

Getting started 9

Expanding your powers of observation 19

Writing to learn 37

Building your personal knowledge library 53

Assessing what you've learned 63

Assessing how you learn 77

Reinforcing positive learning behaviors 89

Tapping into the foundational structure of knowledge 103

Your roadmap to self-discovery 117

Advanced exercises: Expanding your knowledge horizons 123

Afterword 137

Appendix: Resources for diving more deeply into deep learning 141

Index 151

DEEP LEARNING MANUAL

Manifesto

We reject a one-size-fits-all approach to learning. Rather, we encourage each individual to identify ways that reinforce positive learning behaviors and correct negative patterns and tendencies.

While rote learning has its place, guided self-discovery results in better understanding, a greater sense of accomplishment, and a desire to learn more.

People in all stages of learning need to discover problems and solutions on their own, rather than having them dictated by an instructor, textbook, or other authority.

Teachers should not even be asking exam questions. Students should write their own questions, then answer them in ways that express and reinforce the insights they've gained during the discovery process.

When teachers do ask questions, they should be evocative, helping to draw out knowledge (the literal meaning of "educate"), rather than aiming to generate a test score to be rated against some standard or statistical curve.

Handwritten narrative not only promotes learning at a deep structure (memory engram) level, it helps reverse acquired learning disabilities caused by excessive exposure to rote learning and other negative influences.

Mathematics is an excellent way to begin the deep learning process, as it forms a solid foundation for learning and understanding in other disciplines.

Writing about mathematics has to be precise. This carries over into all other disciplines.

Deep learning through guided self-discovery results in not only knowing more about the world, but more importantly, knowing one's self.

The founders and associates of the
Second School Network

Preface

This is the first in a series of manuals aimed at transforming the way we learn. We aren't attempting to introduce some radically new approach. Rather, we aim to re-introduce learning and teaching methods that have been around for centuries, but have slowly fallen out of favor.

The rapid growth of technology and cultural changes of the information age have influenced the way we learn both negatively and positively. On the one hand, easy access to summarized information has reduced the incentive to dive deeply into a subject. People want and often get instant answers without having to go through a long discovery process.

On the other hand, technology opens the door to a whole universe of experiences that are possible only through self-discovery. This means you not only get the satisfaction that comes from solving a problem or challenge on your own, you also learn from and enjoy the innumerable sights, sounds, and ideas you encounter along the way.

Our purpose is to bring these deeper learning experiences back into the mainstream.

The tools, techniques and practices presented here are the products of decades of multi-disciplinary research in the knowledge sciences. Our work began in the 1980s at the University of Texas at Arlington and The George Washington University.

It grew in the 1990s and beyond to include Georgetown University and private research institutions such as the Behavioral Computational Neuropsychology (BCN) Group and the Mountain Quest Institute, whose body of research we continue to draw heavily from today. Finally, through the efforts of the many dedicated researchers and practitioners at Applied Knowledge Sciences, Inc. and the Second School Network, our field work has extended into classrooms and workplaces in various industries across the globe.

The US Army and US Air Force Research Laboratories, the Russian Academy of Sciences, and many other organizations and individuals too numerous to mention collaborated in sponsoring and producing this body of knowledge. The Appendix provides a sampling of foundational publications and other resources.

Our work spans the full spectrum of theory to laboratory development to application in the home, classroom and workplace. Its impact has

PREFACE

been felt across a wide range of subjects and disciplines spanning all aspects of life.

This very much remains a work in progress, in harmony with our central theme of continuous renewal through a lifetime of self-discovery.

We invite you to peel back the curtain and take a look inside. Try the exercises, if only just for fun. Feel free to proceed at your own pace.

You can keep up-to-date and join the discussions at adaptivedeeplearning.com. We welcome your questions, comments, suggestions and constructive criticisms.

DEEP LEARNING MANUAL

Introduction

1

How would you prefer to learn?

There's the usual way. You memorize a bunch of facts, long enough to repeat them on a test. Do that several times a semester, and you'll start racking up course credits. Do it long enough and you'll get a diploma. A certificate. Or a degree. Maybe even a job.

If you end up getting a job you'll be given assignments. Only they won't be anything like the ones you got in school. You'll need to ask somebody how to do them. You'll suddenly realize that you have little or no idea how to apply what you've learned over those many years.

Fortunately, there's a better way, at least in the long run. You won't end up having to cram your head full of empty facts, only to be quickly forgotten. We call the old way *surface learning*, because it's based mostly on what's visible on the surface. The *what*. But very little, if any, of the *why*.

Another way you can learn, really learn, is through a process of guided *self-discovery*. This is what we call *deep learning*.

INTRODUCTION

The idea is simple. When you discover things for yourself, or with a tutor, instructor, or mentor acting as your guide, it "sticks." You gain a deeper understanding of each topic and how to apply it in real life. Even in the presence of new problems and situations you've never encountered.

Isn't that better than passively memorizing just enough to "get by" and move on to the next grade? Or moving up to the next level in your job?

We hope you'll give this second way of learning a try. You'll see it's not only better, it's more fun. You'll experience the joy of discovering things for yourself rather than having somebody else ram them down your throat.

Let's start by re-wiring your brain so you can move from the old "memorize, take the test, and forget" way of learning to the new way. Which, by the way, isn't really new.

2

If you're up for moving from surface-level learning methods like "cram, remember enough to pass the test, then forget," toward a deeper experience, there are a few things you'll need to do. Don't worry. It's pretty simple. Even fun. But it'll mean making a shift in how you think.

The good news is, it's all very low-tech at the outset. Later on we'll fold in technology, but at a level you'll be comfortable with. For now, all you'll need is a #2 pencil and some blank paper. That's pretty much it.

Albert Einstein left the first high school he attended because he hated the rote learning he was subjected to. Many of his greatest discoveries were made not in the laboratory, but with a pad and pencil. He might not have known it, but he was actually applying the same deep learning principles you'll be using here.

We can't promise you'll become the world's next great scientist. But we can promise that if you use these tried and proven techniques, you'll be way ahead of where you would have been had you just memorized a bunch of cold, empty facts. Or spent endless hours sitting in a classroom or in front of a computer screen.

INTRODUCTION

All the great scientists, mathematicians and thinkers in the world went through a process of self-discovery. They spent a great deal of time thinking, reflecting, and writing. Then thinking and reflecting on what they had written. Then writing some more.

Wouldn't you like to experience the same thrill they did, when that flash of insight suddenly appears and everything comes together and makes sense? Which do you think is more satisfying – having somebody give you the answers, or figuring them out for yourself?

3

Whoever heard of taking a class where they don't give you the answers to the questions? And the final exam is a *blank paper test* that doesn't even have any questions?

No, we're not one of those fringe groups that claim there are no right or wrong answers. The difference is, in the world of deep learning, you get to figure them out for yourself.

But how will you know if you have the right answers?

You'll know. And you'll have more confidence than ever in your answers because you'll have opened your mind to your innate and often suppressed ability to reason, which is inherent in all human beings.

You may be confused by what you see going on in the world. Who isn't? The problem is, the world has become so complex that sometimes when you encounter a new problem, you can't just look it up.

But you can be the person who comes up with an innovative solution. And no search engine will ever be able to do that.

INTRODUCTION

That's how to succeed in the 21st century. That's how you'll get ten, even a hundred times more out of your education, work, and life experiences than most.

Get ready, your journey is about to begin...

DEEP LEARNING MANUAL

Getting started

4

How often do you write?

Not emails, word processor documents, text messages, or any of that. We're talking about pencil and paper. Preferably blank paper. With no lines.

In the old days we called it *tabula rasa,* or "clean slate."

When you write with pencil and paper on a blank page you engage your brain in ways that are different from banging away at a keyboard.

Have you ever had a thought or idea and said to yourself, "I'll have to remember that?" Then a short while later you asked, "What was that terrific idea I had?"

Here's something really revolutionary to try. If you don't already have one, go to a bookstore or office supply store and buy a journal.

Don't try to do it on the cheap. Treat yourself to one of those sturdy, leather-bound ones. Or maybe a colorful one with a draw string.

The "cloud" is great for many reasons. But nothing beats pencil and paper.

GETTING STARTED

Sometimes you need to take a break from the cloud. Turn off your tablet PC. And your smartphone. Bring yourself back to something you can not only see, but can touch, feel, and smell. In a real way, not virtually. In your own unique style and signature.

That's how you learn in ways that stick. In ways that excite.

Welcome to the world of deep learning.

Action to take:

Get a journal with unlined blank pages, or a tablet, and several #2 pencils. Always keep them within reach, especially next to your bed.

Get in the habit of writing down thoughts, ideas and insights as soon as they come to mind. It often helps to include the date, time, and place of each entry for future reference.

GETTING STARTED

5

Let's take a closer look at the nearly lost art of writing things out by hand.

Hopefully you have a journal. Or at least something you keep within reach so you can capture your thoughts, ideas and insights about anything and everything.

You might be saying, "Well, I'm not very good at writing." Don't worry. You don't need to be.

In fact, let's just forget about learning to write. Instead, let's flip that whole notion on its head and focus on *writing to learn.*

You see, writing to learn gives you a far better experience than just reading a book, watching a video, or playing a game. Even a so-called "educational" game.

Here's all you need to remember....

First you think of an idea.

Then you observe it, even if it's in your imagination.

Then you think about what you've just observed.

Based on your analysis, you think of what you're going to do next. Then you do it.

Then you think about what you did, and the whole cycle repeats.

The more you apply this process, the smarter you get. But here's the secret ingredient that's so often missing…

You can improve your ability to learn many times over if throughout that whole process you get into the habit of writing things down. It goes something like this…

GETTING STARTED

6

1. Write down your thoughts. About anything. And the stories behind those thoughts. Where did those thoughts and ideas come from?
2. Look for actual or imagined ways those thoughts play out in the world. Write down what you observe – either in actuality or in your imagination. Albert Einstein went through this same process when he asked himself, *"What would it be like to ride on a beam of light?"* The theory of relativity and other world-changing discoveries emerged from that single question.
3. Think about what you've just observed. How do you feel about it? What's unique and why? What's common?
4. Plan a course of action. What would you do to improve or extend your experience? What's the expected outcome? How will you measure it?
5. Do it. Or as some say, "plan the work, then work the plan."
6. Write about your experience. What worked and why? What did you do exceptionally well? What didn't work and why not? How can you make it better? What else can you do, having learned from that experience?

7. Repeat.

It's important to tap into your innermost feelings during this process. No more "check your emotions at the door before entering." Feelings, gut intuition and instinct, along with close observation and in-depth analysis, are the hallmarks of sound decisions.

The same goes for using your imagination. Free-range imagination can lead to real breakthroughs.

Finally, retrospect propels you forward. Knowing what's worked best for you in the past and why, along with what hasn't worked and why not, arms you with the confidence you'll need for the journeys ahead, no matter how difficult they may be.

Follow these seven steps, and a whole new world will open up. If you'll allow it.

GETTING STARTED

Action to take:

If you're like most people, ideas are always popping into your head, usually without warning. Unfortunately, many of those ideas are forever lost because they're not captured.

The next time you think of an idea, grab your journal, or pencil and paper, and write down that idea immediately. You do carry a journal or pad and pencil with you at all times, right?

Expound on that idea using the seven steps outlined earlier in this chapter. It may not amount to anything, or it could cause your life to take off in a whole new direction.

At least from now on those ideas will be there when you need to refer to them. Even if it's years down the road…

DEEP LEARNING MANUAL

Expanding your powers of observation

7

Hopefully by now you have a journal, or at least a notepad, and are beginning to capture your thoughts, ideas, and observations in writing. Here's another technique that'll change the way you learn forever. It's called *descriptive enumeration*.

For now, don't worry about the term or where it comes from. What's important is to get started. Here's an example of how it works.

When you go to the store or other place of business to make a purchase, you're likely to encounter a salesperson or agent. This person will tell you all the wonderful features and benefits of the product or service. This item does this, this item does that, and so on.

In descriptive enumeration, we flip that whole notion around. Instead of having someone tell you what they want you to know, in the exact order they want you to know it, you discover the important aspects for yourself. As they come to mind. Using your own powers of observation.

Before we get started, let's go back to a time when there weren't any written languages. When everything was done in our heads. No word

EXPANDING YOUR POWERS OF OBSERVATION

processors. No search engines. No books. Even before clay tablets.

This means you'll have to put away any pens, pencils, papers, tablets, or keyboards. You'll have to rely solely on memory, with no help from tools or technology. At least for now.

We'll cheat just a little on the technology part and ask you to use a timer. Like the egg timer in your kitchen. Or the digital timer on your mobile phone. It needs to be able to run for 30 to 60 seconds. The timing of the steps in this exercise is critical.

Now think of something you currently own or like. Something that you would normally buy from a salesperson. A blender or other appliance. A sofa or recliner. A car. Even a condo or house. But try to keep it simple.

The item or product you've selected is called the *object of observation*. You'll need to give it a unique name. You decide what to call it.

Once you've given your object of observation a name, you'll mentally construct a series of short, memorable phrases that describe it.

Since you'll be thinking of only one short phrase at a time, your description will certainly not be complete. And since you'll only be given a few moments to think of each phrase, your description may not be totally accurate. But don't worry.

What's important is that you notice what comes to mind first. Above all the clutter. Like a Rorschach test.

All set? You've picked an object of observation? Given it a name? Timer ready? OK, let's go…

EXPANDING YOUR POWERS OF OBSERVATION

8

1. Set the timer for 30 seconds. Start the timer and construct in your mind a short, memorable phrase that says something descriptive about your object of observation. Do this for about 30 seconds, then stop. And remember, no writing!

2. Think about the phrase you've just constructed. Start the timer, and in your mind construct another short phrase that describes the object of observation in a completely different way. Do this for no longer than 30 seconds.

3. Think about the last two phrases you've constructed. Start the timer and think of a third short phrase that describes the object of observation in a way that's completely different from the other two. Do this for about 30 seconds.

4. Now think about your last three descriptive phrases. In your mind, construct another short phrase that describes the object of observation in a way that's completely different from the others. You may need to

stretch a bit, so feel free to extend the time up to 60 seconds, but no more.

5. Continue this process until you've come up with about six to eight short, totally different descriptive phrases. If you're on a roll, keep going. Otherwise you can stop after about half a dozen phrases.

If you're anxious to write down your thoughts, be patient. We'll get to the writing part soon enough.

For now, we're trying to re-awaken the deeper regions of your memory. The parts that record imagery. Sound. Feelings and emotions. Senses like touch, taste, and smell. And most important, the parts that make associations across all of these different aspects.

By not writing down your observations, you're forcing your mind to record them the good old-fashioned way. At a level that sticks. That's why we asked you to think of descriptive phrases that are memorable.

EXPANDING YOUR POWERS OF OBSERVATION

Action to take:

Apply the five descriptive enumeration steps a few more times using different objects of observation. For some real fun, make the object of observation a situation or an event. The same principles will apply.

Keep doing this a little bit every day. Slowly but surely, this new way of thinking will begin to kick in.

It'll change the way you view everything. It'll change the way you learn. It'll rock your world.

9

Hopefully you're having fun practicing descriptive enumeration, your new deep learning technique.

Many of the deep learning methods you'll be using are grounded in mathematics. This is particularly the case with descriptive enumeration.

According to mathematical principles, knowledge about an object, property or event is said to be *canonical* if and only if its descriptive elements are: 1) orthogonal, and 2) complete.

By *orthogonal* we mean that each descriptive phrase is unlike any of the others. One phrase might describe sights. Another, sounds. A third might describe the emotions you feel as an observer: joy, sorrow, fear, and so on.

Complete does not necessarily mean exhaustive. Although it could be, as in the case of relatively simple situations or objects.

But most of our world is quite the opposite. It's so complex that fully complete descriptions would be overwhelming if not impossible.

That's why we consider our knowledge about an object or event to be complete if we have the minimal amount we need to determine the best

EXPANDING YOUR POWERS OF OBSERVATION

course of action to take, given the circumstances. Buy or sell. Fight or flight. Continue negotiating or walk away.

10

Just to be clear, we have nothing against rote learning. Like everything, it has its proper place.

In military academies, boot camps, fraternities and the like, plebes and recruits are pushed through seemingly endless memorization drills. When called upon, they must instantly, loudly, and without hesitation rattle off a litany of mundane items such as the day's breakfast, lunch, and dinner menus. Or the full names and hometowns of each member of their class or company. Or the day's schedule in its entirety.

0600, this happens, in this place. Same for 0715, 0850, and so on. All the way to "lights out." Stumble or make the slightest mistake and push-ups or other humiliating punishments will surely follow.

There's a reason for this. It strengthens short-term memory and along with it, the ability to quickly and accurately recall and communicate detailed facts, observations and instructions to others. In combat or hazardous, rapid-response situations, this could mean the difference between life and death.

EXPANDING YOUR POWERS OF OBSERVATION

Imagine you're under heavy fire. Bombs going off in all directions. Bullets whizzing by, inches above your head. Tactical instructions are coming in over the radio. You can't just stop and say, "Wait a minute, let me grab a pencil and paper!"

While rote memorization is good in the right situation, it should never become the norm. Like cramming your head full of mind-numbing facts and spitting them out on multiple-choice tests.

Or if you're being interviewed by a reporter. Worse yet, if you're a candidate in a political debate. Your advisors insist that no matter what questions you're asked, your response needs to come from a pre-determined set of carefully crafted sound bites. And don't you dare improvise!

This is where the weakness of surface learning becomes all too obvious. As the situations you need to respond to become increasingly complex and challenging, the deeper an understanding you'll need in order to avoid making poor choices.

Bertrand Russel makes the misapplication of rote learning painfully clear in his autobiography where he writes:

> *"I was made to learn by heart: 'The square of the sum of two numbers is equal to the sum of their squares increased by twice their product.' I had not the vaguest*

idea what this meant and when I could not remember the words, my tutor threw the book at my head, which did not stimulate my intellect in any way."

By all means, keep that collection of facts and figures at your fingertips. But for a more fulfilled learning experience, try naming and descriptively enumerating the central topic around which those facts are based.

You'll not only have a much better command of the facts, you'll have a deeper understanding of the meaning behind them, and how they all fit into the big picture.

EXPANDING YOUR POWERS OF
OBSERVATION

Action to take:

Pick something you've learned by rote memory. A "handy dandy" rule of some sort. Or a recipe. A checklist.

Give it a name. Now descriptively enumerate that topic, using the five steps outlined in chapter 8.

What additional insights did you discover about that topic that you didn't appreciate when learning about it from rote memory? Can you think of any circumstances where that simple rule, checklist or recipe would not work?

What can you add to the checklist or recipe to help improve it? If it's a "rule of thumb," how would you modify it, given your expanded view?

11

Think about what you're getting bombarded with on a daily basis. The world is drowning in information. And that information is usually far from orthogonal and nowhere near complete.

If anything, it's a repetitive narrative aimed at getting you to make a pre-determined choice. "Buy this, don't buy that." "Vote for so-and-so." "Support this group, boycott that group." And so on.

Descriptive enumeration broadens your perspective, increasing your powers of observation. You might have heard about incidents where each witness gives a completely different account of what happened. One will portray the event as an accident. Another as intentional. Like a good investigator, you should strive for orthogonality and completeness, especially where important decisions are involved.

But that can be hard to do if deeply entrenched learning behaviors accumulated over a lifetime cause you to look at everything from a single point-of-view. Like when you're programmed to listen passively. To obey the rules. To follow the crowd. To reduce everything down to a simple slogan.

EXPANDING YOUR POWERS OF OBSERVATION

As a human being, you have the capacity for self-discovery through thinking, observing and enumerating. Taking multiple viewpoints into account. Making adjustments and taking action. Then going back to thinking and observing, and repeating the cycle.

This is how great discoveries happen. And there are many more waiting to be made.

Now imagine seven billion minds all around the world doing this.

12

Here's an excellent example of mental enumeration and self-discovery, and the impact it can have on the world…

In the Bloomberg Businessweek article "Being Steve Jobs' Boss," (October 20, 2010) former Pepsi and Apple CEO John Sculley describes how he, Steve Jobs, and Polaroid camera inventor Dr. Edwin Land were sitting at an empty table in a conference room. He noticed that the whole time they were talking, Land and Jobs kept looking at the center of the empty table.

He quotes Land as saying: "I could see what the Polaroid camera should be. It was just as real to me as if it was sitting in front of me before I had ever built one."

To which Jobs replied: "Yeah, that's exactly the way I saw the Macintosh. If I asked someone who had only used a personal calculator what a Macintosh should be like, they couldn't have told me. There was no way to do consumer research on it, so I had to go and create it, and then show it to people, and say now what do you think?"

He recalled that in the meeting, Jobs and Land both said: "These products have always existed—

EXPANDING YOUR POWERS OF OBSERVATION

it's just that no one has ever seen them before. We were the ones who discovered them." That's when Scully realized that both Jobs and Land had the ability not to invent products, but to discover them.

That's a critical distinction. Notice also how the empty table was the centerpiece of their conversation. That's exactly what we've been referring to as *tabula rasa*.

What amazing things already exist in your mind, waiting to be discovered?

DEEP LEARNING MANUAL

Writing to learn

13

By now you should have some topics under your belt. Objects of observation, technically speaking.

You've given each a name. You've mentally gone through the process of descriptive enumeration, coming up with a set of short, descriptive phrases. With each phrase completely unlike the others, your mental image of the object of observation is orthogonal and complete.

Now comes the next step – expressing in writing what you've observed and enumerated in your mind.

Remember, there's a very profound reason for doing it this way. The process of mental enumeration, followed by handwritten narrative, stimulates learning at a deep structure level in memory.

It's also important that your narrative be written on blank, unlined paper. *Tabula rasa,* as we mentioned earlier. This keeps the flow of thoughts free and unencumbered.

Lines and margins are distracting and energy-draining. Did you ever get "dinged" in grade school for going outside the margins? Heaven forbid!

It gets worse in our high-tech world, where much of what you enter on a computer screen has to fit precisely within a standard format. If not – *error message!*

At least for now, you can escape to a different place. Where nobody will bother you about such trivial things.

So grab a #2 pencil and some blank paper. Pick one of the topics you've named and enumerated, and start writing. This is your handwritten expression of what you've learned.

Keep in mind that at this point you're writing for *you* and *you alone*.

For fun, look up images of Isaac Newton's handwritten notes. Or Shakespeare's. Or any of your favorite thinkers, philosophers, writers, architects.

Did any of them really care about making things nice and pretty for an editor? Not in the least. Their purpose was to capture their observations and ideas so they could look back at them reflexively. Learn from them. Be changed by them. Then think about them some more.

What great knowledge explorer is hiding inside of you, waiting to come out? Give this technique a try and find out.

Action to take:

Find images of the handwriting or hand drawings of one of your favorite writers, poets, architects, scientists...anyone of note.

Perform a descriptive enumeration of those images. What do they tell you in general? About how that person thinks or communicates?

What is it about the handwriting or drawing that inspires you? What do you see that points out something you might want to treat cautiously or avoid altogether?

14

Let's talk about what might be a sensitive subject for many. The difficulty or even the inability to write, especially by hand.

The fear of or inability to communicate in writing is more common than you might expect. It's no wonder, given the preponderance of mobile devices we either speak into directly or use by tapping short, cryptic messages onto a touchscreen.

Yet we know that expressing knowledge in written narrative using a pencil and blank paper is many times more effective than passively sitting in class or watching a video. Or reading a book. In fact, handwritten narrative used to be the primary way people learned in the not too distant past.

Prior to the 20th century, most families could not afford to send their children to school. But the lucky few were able to experience learning at a deeper level than is typically experienced in today's classrooms.

They were given plenty of time to read, think, and make observations about the world. Then they were asked to write extensively about what they might do to change things, given the chance. As part of the educated elite, they were quickly able to ascend to positions of power and influence.

Many notable self-taught individuals also reached this level. Benjamin Franklin. Frederick Douglass. Thomas Edison. Abraham Lincoln. Adolph Hitler. Sometimes the changes were for the better. Sometimes for the worse.

Then along came the industrial revolution. Almost by necessity, learning became mechanized, just like the factories where most of the students ended up working.

Next came the information age, which mechanized the flow of information and knowledge. Handwritten notes were replaced by blogs, video clips, sound bites and tweets. Handwritten essays were replaced by term papers you could download and edit using a word processor. Books became fully digitized.

Testing became automated, just like a quality control system on an assembly line. Score a 60 and you pass. 59 and you fail.

Learning became increasingly shallow. So did our capacity to express ourselves. Our primary means of communication became short e-mails, text messages loaded with shorthand and acronyms, or simple snapshots.

Where are you on this spectrum? Do words magically flow onto the page? Or haven't you written anything by hand in years, save for a few notes taped to the bottom of your computer screen?

15

Maybe at some point you just stopped writing altogether. Especially if it didn't seem to matter. You were always passed on to the next grade anyway.

Or maybe you're one of the many who are simply unable to tell a story or explain something in handwritten form. If for some reason you had to do it on short notice, it could be downright embarrassing.

Not to worry. You can start from anywhere, even if it's with only a few scribbled lines. But start you must. Just remember that at least for now, you're expressing knowledge solely for yourself.

So have fun! Draw cartoons. Make up your own symbols.

Or dust off an old grade school book on writing and start practicing. Get a retired person to help you – they'd love to do it!

It doesn't matter which way you choose. What's important is that you choose a way and start doing it.

Perhaps you're at the other end of the spectrum. Maybe you're one of those people who has used every word in the Oxford English Dictionary in a sentence at least once. You were probably chastised in school, maybe even bullied, because your writing was incomprehensible to the "general population."

If this is you, great. Write away. Fill those pages with all the big words you can muster. As long as – and this is critical – your narrative represents your best expression of the descriptive enumeration exercise you went through for the topic under study.

Whichever end of the spectrum you are, or if you're somewhere in the middle, start filling up those journal pages. Or to put it in the words of pop artist Madonna as she confidently belts out one of her legendary hits…"*Express Yourself!*"

Action to take:

A great way to get into the habit of writing things out by hand is to write a note to someone. Use one of those greeting cards with no pre-printed message on the inside, just a blank space. It's a great way to say, "thank you," or "thinking of you," or "I just wanted to share this with you."

It has a powerful impact on a number of levels, both for you the sender, and for the recipient.

16

Fear has tremendous power, especially when it comes to setting up barriers to learning. It plays a major role in keeping both students and people in the workforce from reaching their full potential.

It can be fear of the subject itself. This is often the case in mathematics. It could be the fear of being looked down upon by one's peers. Or the fear of making a mistake. Or of looking dumb or foolish.

The following story shows one of the many types of transformations that are possible when you break deeply entrenched patterns and journey into the realm of guided self-discovery.

It's told by a college mathematics professor who uses deep learning methods in the classroom. It's a story of how the fear of failure kept a college algebra student from realizing his full potential, and the breakthrough that occurred once that fear was conquered…

> *"In my classroom students wrote a narrative-type exam in class every four weeks. We had no textbooks, since the college was close to bankruptcy and the bookstore had been closed down. Instead, we*

relied on my familiarity of what was supposed to be covered in a college algebra class.

"One of the students was utterly unable to demonstrate that he was connecting with the concepts we were studying. He was always the first to arrive and last to leave the classroom. He always sat next to the door in a class of forty students. He was shy and on an autism scale would be rated as slightly autistic. He was well liked by his peers, but stayed to himself.

"Each time this student turned in a 'blank paper test', there were only lightly drawn short marks. You could turn the paper sideways or upside down, and nothing was readable as something even close to clear handwriting.

"However, in class I would occasionally turn to him and ask him a question. He generally had the right answer. He was just unable to write an exam. So I graded him on his class performance. He earned a 'C' that semester and was enrolled in the second semester of liberal arts mathematics.

"I kept expecting this student's blank paper test to start to show real symbols in English and mathematics. But it was like playing 'hide and seek.' I pointed to a part of his paper, one day, and said, 'See there, you did write it.' His response was to deny that anything was written on the paper.

"This was very odd. He worked on the sheets of paper with great attention. But always he turned in a collection of six to ten sheets of paper with random pencil scratches that were lightly drawn. One could almost not see them.

"Two tests before the end of the second semester, he started to show fear that he would not pass. I told him that I had already assigned a grade of 'C' and that this would be his last math class. I told him to enjoy being here.

"His written test before the final exam was like all the others. Lovely art, but with no assigned meaning, at least that I could see. I smiled and said 'thank you' when he turned in his stack of papers.

"Then the day of the final exam came. All of the students except him started the test session on time.

"I passed out blank paper with no instructions. They each knew what to do. Each student started to work on expressing what he or she had learned in class that year.

"The last student to arrive was this young man. His usual place was occupied, so he moved to the back.

"As he passed by me, I handed him ten sheets of unlined paper. I watched as he sat down with only a pencil and these blank sheets of paper. During the

exam, he worked as he always did, leaning over his paper making marks.

"*Towards the end of the testing period, with at least five students still working, he walked up to my desk and handed me the ten sheets of paper. In his own handwriting, written in a way that was easily readable, he had presented the topics of the two-semester college algebra course. Glancing over the pages took me just a few moments.*

"*It was perfect! He had made a coherent presentation using all the right symbols. He had made up examples of topics and moved through the curriculum in a way that conveyed to me that he understood the material.*

"*I glanced up and told him that he just earned an 'A' in his last math class. He turned, and I thought I saw him float to the door. No sounds, just floating.*

"*Had I not seen this type of thing before, I would have not handled it right. The point is that my expectation was that he was in fact learning, and learning deeply; but that he had been unable to communicate this on the tests.*

"*His fear of not passing was part of the barrier. Once this fear was removed, the proper expression was realized.*"

17

Take a moment and think about what might be holding you back. Maybe it's something a teacher or some other person said to you long ago that you still can't seem to shake loose.

Be assured, you're not alone. Multi-billionaire and Chairman of the 400-company Virgin Group Sir Richard Branson was told by the headmaster of his school that he would either end up in jail or become a millionaire. But neither that nor dyslexia could stop him from literally reaching for the stars as he's now doing with *Virgin Galactic*.

Many other successful people have similar stories. Our research has shown that prolonged exposure to teaching methods focusing on the surface level can actually create a learning disability where one previously didn't exist. Practicing deep learning on a regular basis will help propel you in the opposite direction.

By the way, it's well-known that Richard Branson always carries a notepad and pencil with him. In meetings he frowns upon slide presentations and has a reputation for being a voracious note taker. With more than four hundred companies to watch over, he must be doing something right.

DEEP LEARNING MANUAL

Building your personal knowledge library

18

In this next leg of your deep learning journey you'll need to build a *knowledge space*. It's a way to visually organize and represent the topics in your growing body of knowledge, including subject headings and categories.

Remember when we asked you to give each topic you were enumerating a name? That name is the label which identifies every topic, every object of observation, you create. It also allows you to put a topic into a particular category so you can refer to it later. Just like books on a shelf or file folders in a drawer.

A knowledge space can be built using many different structures and formats. It could be a list, such as a table of contents, subject index, or outline. It could be visual, like a mind map or conceptual graph. Or something like a bubble diagram.

A white board or a wall with a sticky surface works up to a point. But this is where you'll need to start using technology to organize, maintain, and link your growing collection of handwritten notes.

BUILDING YOUR PERSONAL KNOWLEDGE LIBRARY

The Appendix contains a list of some of the knowledge mapping tools we've used. Choose the method and tool that works best for you.

You may want to use more than one tool. That's fine, as long as the tools are linked together so that every unique topic appears in every tool (not an easy thing to do, so you might want to start with only one).

Here's a list of some of the more popular types of tools available:

___ Visual mapping tools (mind maps, etc.)

___ Wikis

___ Blogs

___ Word processors (must be able to create and maintain an index)

Whichever tool you choose, five distinct characteristics must be present. You must be able to:

1. Assign a unique name or label to each topic
2. Place the topics into categories and sub-categories
3. Link topics to show important associations (such as "A" is a part of "B," or "A" is a type of "B")

4. Attach scanned copies of your handwritten notes from your descriptive enumeration exercises, class notes, and blank paper tests to the appropriate topics
5. Easily search and navigate the content.

You can organize and sort your topics and categories however you like: alphabetically, by date, by importance, etc. Remember, it's *your* private knowledge space.

It's one thing if you're in charge of arranging the shelves in a bookstore or library. There you have to comply with a one-size-fits-all standard so people can quickly find what they're looking for.

The Library of Congress Card Catalog system was designed for this purpose. Business books go in a certain location. Cooking, herb gardening, travel, mystery, each have their own place.

But a knowledge space is your creation. Organize it in the way that works best for you. Like the way you organize your hard drive. Your toolbox. Your purse. Your closet. Only now you should be able to do even better!

Get started by picking a tool and assembling your collection of topics and categories. You'll quickly begin to experience the deep satisfaction that

BUILDING YOUR PERSONAL KNOWLEDGE LIBRARY

comes from designing, building and growing your own unique body of knowledge.

At that point you may even want to start sharing it with others. If you do, be ready for the floodgates to really open up.

Action to take:

Go to the "Knowledge spaces and learning spaces" section in the Appendix. Check out the links to the various tools for creating and growing a knowledge space.

The Appendix only provides a few examples, so feel free to research as many of the more than one hundred tools available. Pick one and start building out your knowledge space.

If you choose one that's not listed as an example and it works well for you, please let us know at adaptivedeeplearning.com/contact.htm so we can share your recommendation with the rest of the community.

BUILDING YOUR PERSONAL KNOWLEDGE LIBRARY

19

One comment we keep hearing is: "This is really hard."

Yes, it's hard. It has to be if you're going to have a deep understanding of what's going on in the world. You'll need to know not only the *what*, but the *who, when, where, why,* and *how* as well. And that's going to take much more effort than just memorizing a bunch of facts and rules.

With that in mind, let's do another descriptive enumeration exercise – this time where it really counts.

This may be one of the most important descriptive enumerations of your entire life.

The object of observation is *learning*. Not someone else's idea of learning. We're talking about learning as you see it through your own eyes. As you sense it. Experience it.

As always, begin by giving this object of observation a name. Call it whatever you like. It's your choice entirely.

Next comes the part where, in 30- to 60-second intervals, you think of short, memorable phrases that describe your perception of learning. No writing. At least not yet. Keep your pencil and blank paper or journal out of reach for the moment.

Think of a descriptive phrase. Make it short and memorable. Now think of another phrase that's completely different. Then another. And another. Each one totally different from the rest.

There's no need to cover everything. Overthinking is incompatible with deep learning.

Let the thoughts flow naturally. Whatever comes to mind in the span of a few minutes.

All finished? How was it? Hard? Maybe. It takes effort. That's because you're using your brain in ways which may be totally unfamiliar.

Don't worry, you'll get used to it. And it'll definitely be worth it.

Now comes the writing part...

BUILDING YOUR PERSONAL KNOWLEDGE LIBRARY

20

Grab your pencil and blank paper. Or your journal. Express in writing, the topic of learning.

Start with the name you've given it. Then write down your descriptive enumeration phrases.

Elaborate. Tell stories. Share your innermost feelings. Bare your soul. Write about your learning triumphs and disasters.

Still not comfortable with writing? Then *draw*. Use sketches. Stick figures. Cartoons. Diagrams. Whatever works. Try different things.

Keeping a journal is best. You'll enjoy periodically looking back and seeing how your view of learning has evolved over time.

Always keep your journal within easy reach. This gets you into the habit of capturing ideas as soon as they pop into your head. Even when you've consciously halted the descriptive enumeration process, it's still running in the background. And every now and then…BAM! A new flash of insight will suddenly hit.

When that happens, you'll want to instantly write it down, preferably alongside the entries you're making right now. Like panning for gold, over time those valuable nuggets will accumulate and grow into a treasure trove of deep knowledge.

We'll return to your narrative shortly. What you're writing now will form the baseline for your deep learning assessment both on the topic of learning as well as your own learning patterns, behaviors and tendencies.

Soon you'll start seeing yourself in an entirely new light.

Assessing what you've learned

21

Slowly but surely you should be getting into the habit of writing down your thoughts on a blank sheet of paper. Capturing and making a permanent record of your insights about a topic. Something you've observed going on in the world. Or in your imagination.

A bound journal works best. It's your personal index to the growing body of knowledge you're building. Each entry is the result of descriptively enumerating in your mind the various orthogonal aspects of an object of observation.

Now comes the point we talked about earlier, where Einstein, Newton and all the great thinkers looked back at their handwritten notes and learned from them. As their notes became their teacher, more thoughts and ideas followed. Descriptive enumerations kept flowing, sometimes extending into totally unrelated areas.

We call this point in the deep learning cycle the assessment phase. It consists of two parts.

The first is determining the extent of your knowledge about the topic and your progress in learning it. How shallow or how deep is your knowledge? How broad or how narrow?

ASSESSING WHAT YOU'VE LEARNED

The purpose here is to figure out where you are relative to where you want to be. Or to put it in terms of an old expression, "you can't get to where you're going if you don't know from where you're starting."

The second part of assessment deals with how well you are learning about how to learn. In many ways this part is just as important as the first. It provides an indication of what learning behaviors, positive and negative, are at work and what adjustments, if any, need to be made.

22

The first part of assessment helps determine where you need to focus your efforts in exploring a given topic, and whether or not you're ready to move on to another.

There are many elaborate, comprehensive assessment tools and methods available. The problem with applying such methods is you can quickly get caught in the trap of attempting to do too much. It's important not to get lost in details which may have no bearing on the context in which a topic is being investigated.

Four these reasons, we've narrowed this part of the assessment process down to four top-level criteria:

- Skill
- Synthesis
- Evaluativeness
- Completeness.

Skill is a measure of your understanding of a topic or subject. Your written narrative is a reflection of your command of the terminology and how well you understand the basic principles. "Topic x consists of a, b, c, and d. Here's what each aspect means and how it's used." The quality of the examples in your narrative, including storytelling, should reveal progressively increasing skill levels.

Your skill level is also an indicator of your ability to apply basic principles of the topic to solve certain types of problems. For example, a maintenance technician's troubleshooting skill level can be indicated by the ability to match a variety of symptoms with known solutions.

For reasons we've mentioned earlier, you should avoid using numeric scores. Instead, pick a range of simple qualitative measures such as "beginner, intermediate, advanced."

Don't get too bogged down trying to decide what assessment criteria to use. Since this is primarily a self-assessment process, pick a scale you're comfortable with. You'll know better than anyone else if you're a "raw beginner," or an "ace."

Don't be too hard on yourself, or too easy. Just be honest.

While skill can exist at both the surface and deep knowledge levels, *synthesis* is primarily characteristic of deep learning. In synthesis you're looking for evidence of your ability to anticipate and solve unforeseen problems by combining different aspects of the topic in novel ways.

Because we promote self-discovery, *evaluativeness* is also a critical factor. Your evaluativeness with respect to a particular topic is indicated by your capacity and willingness to pose and answer progressively more difficult and complex questions and problem statements. In other words, your ability to "stretch" the boundaries of your knowledge about the topic. This is where the blank paper test we mentioned earlier provides an assessment superior to that of a multiple choice standardized test.

People with a high degree of evaluativeness in a subject are able to formulate increasingly challenging *"what if"* scenarios. As such, they play a major role in helping organizations plan, prepare for and respond to a wide range of contingencies.

The more you're willing to stretch reflects the confidence you have in your understanding of the topic. This will come into play later when we assess learning behaviors.

Finally, *completeness* is evidence that your exploration into a topic has revealed all the aspects necessary to make sound decisions, given the context in which the topic is to be applied. It doesn't mean trying to see how many facts about a topic you can cram into your head.

Rather, deep learning develops the ability to derive a minimal set of attributes and actions needed to understand and solve a specific category of problems within a bounded set of circumstances. This factor has tremendous payoff potential for effective decision-making in critical situations, especially where time is of the essence.

Action to take:

Build your initial assessment rubric. We say "initial" because you'll definitely want to make refinements along the way.

For each of the four assessment criteria listed below, develop a qualitative scale of measurement. Use at least three but no more than five points on the scale, ranging from lowest to highest.

Use a word or short phrase to label each point. If it helps, write a brief description for each point on the scale. But it's best if your metrics are self-explanatory and easily understood.

Skill:
- (lowest):
- (optional):
- (medium):
- (optional):
- (highest):

Synthesis:
- (lowest):
- (optional):
- (medium):
- (optional):

ASSESSING WHAT YOU'VE LEARNED

- (highest):

Evaluativeness:
- (lowest):
- (optional):
- (medium):
- (optional):
- (highest):

Completeness:
- (lowest):
- (optional):
- (medium):
- (optional):
- (highest):

23

Narrative-based assessment has the potential to dramatically transform education. Focusing only on whether you pass or fail too often results in fear, intimidation, and discouragement.

Handwritten notes and blank paper tests are extremely effective in promoting learning by helping to spot both stumbling blocks and opportunities for improvement. They help you make the right adjustments so you can learn at progressively deeper levels. This is feedback that extends far beyond what you get from a standard qualifying test or a typical final exam.

As your knowledge approaches the level of mastery, you'll gain the ability to both expand and retract your knowledge horizon. This is technically called "*scatter and gather*," another technique to stimulate learning at a deep level.

As you develop a rich set of topics and subtopics and their descriptive enumerations, try re-arranging them into different clusters and changing how they are associated. "Shuffling the deck," if you will. Many of these new associations and categorizations won't make any sense, but every now and then…

ASSESSING WHAT YOU'VE LEARNED

24

Let's take a look at how assessment and knowledge spaces work together.

Knowledge spaces organize topics into categories, using links to show how those topics and categories are related. They also play a critical role in helping you keep track of your learning progress.

Ideally, you'll want to arrange your knowledge space to visually indicate three types of topics: 1) topics you know; 2) topics you don't know; 3) topics you need to explore more deeply. You may use any type of icon or visual indicator you like.

For topics you know, you'll want to include an indicator that measures the depth of your knowledge using the four-part assessment rubric (skill, synthesis, evaluativeness and completeness).

If some of the topics in this category are part of your ongoing exploration, then the assessment rubric should tell you where you are and where you need to be. The gap between these two measures helps you determine your *learning objectives*.

For topics you don't know, you can leave them unmarked. Or you might want to flag those you might need for future reference.

The third type consists of topics that you'll need to learn in the future, either as part of a planned curriculum, or as part of your personal lifelong learning strategy. The part of your knowledge space that represents what you know and what you need to know is called your *learning space*.

It's important to note that the path to getting to what you need to know should not be rigid, as is often the case with traditional education. In the world of deep learning, you're free to wander.

If you keep an open mind, you'll continually discover new topics to add to your learning and knowledge spaces. There may be other topics you'll want to either discard or move from "need to know" to "possible future reference."

One thing is for certain. You'll no longer have to plow through 500-page textbooks. We're talking totally customized learning. Flexible and adaptive. The way learning ought to be.

ASSESSING WHAT YOU'VE LEARNED

Action to take:

Whether you're using a visual map, outline, or other form for your knowledge space, think of a suitable way to label the topics and group them into the following three categories:

- known
- not known
- need to know more.

You can do this initially by using your best judgment. Ideally, you should use the four-part assessment rubric you developed in chapter 22.

DEEP LEARNING MANUAL

Assessing how you learn

25

Let's take a look at the second part of assessment, learning how to learn. We've already discussed determining how well you've learned a topic under investigation, using skill, synthesis, evaluativeness, and completeness as metrics. Now we'll look into assessing *learning behaviors* and what adjustments, if any, you'll need to make in order to improve the learning process.

How you learn evolves over a lifetime of habits and beliefs you pick up and internalize along the way. The conditioning process begins in pre-kindergarten and continues through the workplace into retirement.

An all too common result of the steady reinforcement of surface-level learning behaviors is what we call an *acquired learning disability*.

Most people equate the term "learning disability" with a psychological or neurological condition such as Asperger's, dyslexia, or ADHD. But learning disabilities can also come from prolonged exposure to poor learning practices and other negative influences. One such disability is the loss of a person's innate desire to investigate and explore.

ASSESSING HOW YOU LEARN

You might recall that phase in early childhood when you kept asking, "Why? Why? Why?" Unless you were fortunate enough to be around patient and understanding adults, your curiosity was likely to be systematically dampened as you grew accustomed to hearing the words, "Shut up!" Or, "Because I say so!" Or, "You'll find out when you get older!"

Think back to your pre-school and elementary school days. Some of the more important matters on your mind were things like, "When do we eat?" Or, "When can we go out and play?"

As a child you quickly learn that somebody else – your parent, teacher, babysitter – decides when, where and what you eat and play. What you watch. What music you listen to.

Then it's on to middle school, high school and college. There you're asking, "What questions will be on the exam?" "What courses do we need to pass in order to graduate?"

Just as in grade school, somebody – a teacher, guidance counselor, advisor – tells you what you need to do. You've become an adolescent child.

You finally enter the workforce. By now, you've been conditioned to avoid asking hard, or worse yet, sensitive questions. You've turned off that wide-eyed explorer self, and know just the right questions to ask. Questions like, "Okay boss, what do you want me to do?" Or "How am I supposed to do this?"

And those dreaded final exams? They've been replaced by those equally dreaded performance reviews. Welcome to the world of the adult child.

ASSESSING HOW YOU LEARN

26

It doesn't stop there. Now that you have a job, the consumer child starts coming out. News and advertising media become your supervisors. "What kind of car should I buy?" "How can I lose weight?" "How big a house can I afford?" "For whom should we vote?"

Eventually you might get promoted and become a manager yourself. But don't worry, in the mind of your employer, you're still a child. You find yourself asking, "How much of a raise should we give everybody?" "Whom do we lay off?" "What payments do we defer until next quarter?"

As you rise through the ranks, the people in authority become increasingly more obscure. Words like "the Committee," "the Board," or even the more nebulous and unaccountable "system," become part of the vocabulary.

As you approach and eventually enter retirement, those hard-wired behaviors remain firmly in-place. You become the senior child. Your bosses are many: your financial planner; your doctor; the government.

"What stocks should I buy? "Where are interest rates headed?" "Should I take out a reverse mortgage?" "When can I retire?" "Will I need surgery?"

Of course, your parents, teachers, peers, bosses, and elected leaders all mean well. They'd never want to deliberately reduce your learning capacity. Yet that's exactly what happens over the years.

Clearly, you need the advice of experienced people. You shouldn't just click through a few web pages and then make an important decision. Yet that's what many people do.

Recognizing the existence of these patterns is in itself a huge step. And yes, the system is deeply entrenched. Push too hard and you'll get burned. Your account canceled. Your membership revoked. Your application denied.

No matter where you are in life, now's the time to start re-wiring your brain. Opening up your mind to new and expanded patterns of learning. It may take a while, but it'll be well worth the effort in the long run.

Next, we'll look more closely at good and bad learning behaviors and how to spot them.

ASSESSING HOW YOU LEARN

27

Successful knowledge transfer depends in large part on understanding learning behaviors. This goes for the classroom, the workplace, and life in general.

Some people like to sit and listen, taking things in verbally. Others respond to lots of movement and emotion. Others prefer diagrams and flowcharts. The type of knowledge space you've selected and how you're populating it, including your use of colors, textures, etc., provide clues as to which learning behaviors are at work in your own life.

Certain types of learning behaviors play an important role in mainstream education. Beginning in the early grades, teachers keep an eye open for warning signs such as an inability to focus, constant fidgeting, withdrawal, and the like. Some of these behaviors may indicate the presence of learning disabilities such as dyslexia. So it pays to be on the lookout.

But many of the behaviors teachers are looking for tend to deal with surface-level, as opposed to deep, learning. When negative traits and tendencies are identified, instructors often respond by trying to force a change.

They might say in a loud voice, "Pay attention!" Or, "Stay after class and write this out on the board." Images of the cartoon character Bart Simpson come to mind.

But instead of treating the symptoms, we need to become more attuned to behaviors that signal the potential for developing and improving deep learning practices. These can have the greatest impact in the long run.

Raising your own self-awareness of these signals is key. You know yourself better than anyone else. Let's take a closer look at what to look for and why.

Action to take:

What people, events, or other factors have influenced your approach to learning:

- in a positive way:

- in a negative way:

28

Learning how to learn means knowing how well you think, observe, enumerate, express, assess and adjust. Your attitudes and behaviors at each of these six steps will in large part determine how shallow or deep your learning experience will be.

It's important to recognize that there are two worlds when it comes to learning: your inner world and your outer world. Your inner world is made up of things like your own self-talk. Your imagination. What you dream about.

Your outer world consists of the physical learning environments you occupy and the people with whom you interact. The classroom. Workplace. Home. Car. Coffee shop.

The root cause of many learning difficulties can be traced in large part to the gap between these two worlds. Some experiences straddle both. Your playlist or home DVD library is an example. Although it's mostly made up of artifacts constructed by others, you decide the time, the place, and the order in which you listen.

What if you could put together a learning list the same way you do a play list? What would it look like? Why not build one and find out?

ASSESSING HOW YOU LEARN

Action to take:

1. Go back to your knowledge space and look over the topics labeled:
   - not known
   - need to know more.

   From these two groups, select the topics you want to explore next, and highlight them in some way. This will constitute your learning space.

2. Start assessing your personal learning behaviors by asking yourself the following pairs of questions. Each pair compares where you are with where you want to be:

What do you like to learn?	What do you spend most of your time learning?
How do you like to learn?	How do you do most of your learning?

DEEP LEARNING MANUAL

When and where do you like to learn?	When and where does most of your learning take place?
From whom do you wish to learn?	From whom do you learn now?
Why do you want to learn?	Is your current learning responding to that need?
How intense is your desire to learn?	Is your current learning occurring at that same level of intensity?

3. Based on your answers to the above pairs of questions, where are the greatest gaps between your desires and your actual learning experience?

4. How can you begin to close those gaps?

Reinforcing positive learning behaviors

29

The way you express what you've learned impacts what you learn and how well you learn it.

You might want to read that sentence again.

How well you learn is a reflection of what's going on at a deep level. That's a far cry from observing the blank expressions or eye movements which often appear when reciting something from memory.

The next step in your deep learning journey is getting into the habit of reading what you've written. Thinking about the content. Paying attention to the underlying signals.

As they say, "success leaves clues." Your handwritten notes are loaded with clues about what's going on deep beneath the surface. They can be the same as, or even more revealing than, looking at yourself in a mirror.

Step back for a minute and take a look at your handwriting. What do you see? What does it tell you about your innermost self? Your thought processes? Your attitudes and biases? Your state of mind?

REINFORCING POSITIVE LEARNING BEHAVIORS

What emotions are screaming at you in a loud voice? Which ones are barely audible, but desperately trying to come out?

It takes practice, but try to examine both the handwriting features and the content together. And no, we're not talking about performing handwriting analysis at the level of, say, a forensic investigation. For now, just use your own best judgment when it comes to assessing your handwriting.

As anyone who keeps a journal knows, this can be lots of fun. Especially when you go back and re-read your entries years, even decades, later.

30

Here are some things to look for…

- Does your handwritten narrative indicate fear or confidence?
- What does it reveal about your ability to handle complexity?
- Does it reflect an ability to connect the dots? To string different concepts together?
- Does it indicate a desire to adhere to certain boundaries and limitations, or a willingness to "stretch?"
- How much of your narrative, if any, contains questions?
- To what extent does your narrative, including both writing style and penmanship, convey emotion?
- Does your writing indicate confidence, fear, or anxiety?
- Strong belief or cynicism?
- Logical organization or free-spirit randomness?
- What degree of patience or impatience is indicated?
- Does it show a desire to keep diving ever more deeply, or to quickly halt once a

REINFORCING POSITIVE LEARNING BEHAVIORS

certain threshold of understanding is reached?
- Does it indicate a positive or negative self-image?
- Does it indicate a positive or negative image of the subject matter? Of the instructor, coach, or mentor? Of your peers? Of yourself?
- Does it come across as goal-oriented or journey-oriented?

Since these are questions you answer yourself, some would argue that they're prone to bias. If you tend to be hard on yourself, there will likely be a negative slant. If you tend to go easy on yourself, your assessment might be overly optimistic.

For now, let's not worry about bias. The fact that you're even asking these questions will cause you to think about learning habits in new ways.

You don't need to take on all of these aspects in one sitting. Start slowly. See which ones jump out at you initially. Then expand your view, a little at a time.

Action to take:

Pick a handwritten descriptive enumeration narrative from one of the exercises. Using your best judgment, answer the questions in the bullet list above.

What do your answers reveal to be your greatest strengths?

Your greatest areas for improvement?

REINFORCING POSITIVE LEARNING BEHAVIORS

31

You might say, "I don't have the foggiest idea how to do handwriting analysis. How am I supposed to tell whether my handwriting indicates things like fear or confidence? Simplicity or complexity?"

The answer is that deep inside, you actually can tell. And by now you should know how to do it.

That's right. By performing a descriptive enumeration exercise on handwriting.

This is exactly how deep learning works. It works for handwriting. For science and mathematics. For learning about learning. For your toughest subject. Your greatest fear. Your greatest passion.

Action to take:

Do a descriptive enumeration exercise on the topic of handwriting. Do the mental enumeration first, followed by a handwritten narrative on blank paper.

After you've completed the exercise, use what you've come up with as a guide to analyzing your own handwriting.

Build out an area in your knowledge space around the subject of handwriting analysis. Use the insights from this exercise to help you with your self-assessment and to make any needed adjustments in your learning space.

REINFORCING POSITIVE LEARNING BEHAVIORS

32

You might be wondering exactly what you should do after you've performed an assessment. One possible outcome is you may have determined that you have a sense of dread, even disdain, for a particular topic.

Take mathematics, for example. An indicator might be that your passion for the topic (one of the assessment questions) is extremely low.

One way to address disdain, disillusionment or even plain old disinterest is to set that topic aside for a moment and take a look at what you're most passionate about. And you definitely know how to do this…by doing a descriptive enumeration exercise on your passion!

Not the focus of your passion. We're talking about passion itself.

How do you recognize passion? What do you feel? Don't worry about what self-help books or other people have told you. This is your own personal enumeration of passion.

Action to take:

Do a descriptive enumeration exercise on the topic of passion. Then write a narrative about your observations. Include stories of what triggers passion in you. What fires you up. Or what you've observed in others.

Add this topic to your knowledge space and make it an ongoing object of observation.

REINFORCING POSITIVE LEARNING BEHAVIORS

33

Now let's find a way to connect a disdained topic to your passion. It's easier than you might think.

Let's say you're an artist, a dancer, a musician – someone who's passionate about the arts.

You're required to take two semesters of college algebra, which you hate. The question people in this situation usually ask is, "what do I need to do in order to survive and escape with a passing grade?" This is obviously a poor quality question.

Instead, try asking a better, higher quality question. Such as, "How can I turn these mathematics courses into an experience that will make me a better artist? A better musician? A better writer? A better thinker?"

This may sound a bit hokey at first. But stay with us. Really, how can you turn mathematics into an art?

You may not see a direct connection right away. So look for indirect ones. For example, achieving excellence in any art form requires a great deal of creative thought. And guess what? So does mathematics!

Spend some time thinking about how mathematics can help you become a better, more creative thinker. Maybe it's by helping you to think more clearly. More broadly. More deeply. Or any number of other ways.

STEM (Science, Technology, Engineering and Mathematics) majors and graduates, in general, tend to think logically, in terms of subjects and predicates. Conditions and outcomes. That's why traditional math pedagogy often suits them just fine.

But most people don't realize that mathematics is really more art than science. Much more. It has elegance and beauty. Symmetry and asymmetry. Even texture.

If you're artistically inclined, this could actually give you an advantage over the so-called "geeks." Precious few math professors realize this.

This is what education is really all about.

REINFORCING POSITIVE LEARNING BEHAVIORS

Action to take:

Give this mind-shift exercise a try. Not only for mathematics but for all your areas of study. Including those you like and those you don't like.

DEEP LEARNING MANUAL

Tapping into the foundational structure of knowledge

34

Even though we've been talking about learning at a deep structure level for some time, you might be wondering: "What exactly is deep structure?"

The good news is that deep knowledge structures are simple and elegant. Just like mathematics!

They're like the stratified layers of rock deep beneath the Earth's surface. You know they're there but you can't really see them.

But you can model them. Diagram them. Describe them in various ways, using color, texture, and a host of other attributes.

The same goes for deep knowledge. Deep knowledge resides in two places: in nature's intelligence, and deep in human memory. At what we call the *engram* level.

How are deep structures revealed? By using the exact same deep learning cycle we've been talking about. By thinking, observing, enumerating, expressing, assessing, and adjusting.

All the great thinkers did this. Much of our work is founded on their insights and discussions. A list of resources and studies we've drawn upon

TAPPING INTO THE FOUNDATIONAL STRUCTURE OF KNOWLEDGE

over the years in our research is provided in the Appendix.

It would take many volumes to completely enumerate this vast body of work and how we're applying it. We hope to bring out more in future books.

For now, here's a simple model that has withstood the test of time. *Time-invariant*, as we like to say. That model is the *threefold structure of knowledge...*

35

All knowledge consists of three and only three dimensions: 1) observer; 2) observed; 3) observation. In more general terms, a subject, an object, and a process (how the subject and object interact). That's it.

All three need to be present. Anything more is unnecessary and fundamentally incorrect. Anything less and the knowledge is fragmented and incomplete, which often gets us into trouble.

Think of the contrast between Eastern and Western philosophies. In Eastern thought, the subjective aspect of knowledge has primacy. You'll hear expressions like, "the inner self." The "seer." Internal, subjective experience. In its most extreme forms, all externality is suspect, not to be trusted. Truth resides only within.

In the West, knowledge is typically approached from the opposite direction. In applying the scientific method, for example, subjectivity is frowned upon in the interest of purely "objective" science.

In Eastern approaches, the goal is to have the observer completely free of any influence of what's being observed. In the West, the flip side

TAPPING INTO THE FOUNDATIONAL STRUCTURE OF KNOWLEDGE

is true. The object of observation must be totally "blind" to the observer.

Only recently in quantum physics, with principles such as entanglement, have people begun to accept that such isolation is impossible. That you cannot observe something without changing it, and without having it change you. That's the interaction, or middle part of this threefold structure coming into play, with all three acting as one.

This is what we referred to earlier when we talked about how the great thinkers reflexively looked back on their handwritten notes. Reflexivity is a key part of the interplay between subject and object. Observer and observed.

To focus only on the subject and not the object, or vice versa, and not include the interaction between the two, results in fragmented, incomplete knowledge. And with that comes errors. Sometimes minor, sometimes catastrophic.

Remember how Galileo was sentenced to prison by the Catholic Church? The Church maintained that man was the center of creation. That was the subjective element coming out.

Galileo and future astronomers argued that we were really specs of cosmic dust on this little rock whirling around the sun, which was in turn whirling around the center of the galaxy, which was in turn whirling around the universe with a hundred billion other galaxies.

Guess what? Both are right. Look at the sky at night. A connection is established in which you change that distant star and that very star changes you.

And that's the case for every observer and every object that's being observed. From the tiniest particles in the Large Hadron Collider at CERN to the massive galaxies at the edge of the universe seen by the Hubble Space Telescope, this threefold structure of knowledge is an invariant. It'll always be there as you continue on your journey. It'll serve as a reminder not to, as the Church and Galileo did, get stuck in only one way of viewing the world.

TAPPING INTO THE FOUNDATIONAL STRUCTURE OF KNOWLEDGE

Action to take:

Think of something or someone you've observed or have interacted with.

How did that activity change you, the subject?

How did it change the object of your observation or interaction?

How did it change the process of how you and the object observe or interact?

36

We've only given you a tiny glimpse into the world of deep structure. In the era of big data, with innumerable zettabytes swirling around, it's easy to lose sight of the fact that there are time-invariant structures at the heart of it all.

The threefold structure of observer, observed, and observation is one such invariant. It represents a stable structure underneath all the perceived chaos.

The human brain has a similar deep structure. At the root of human memory are basic elements called engrams.

Atoms are another type of basic element. Subjected to the natural laws of valence, they can only be combined in certain ways. Yet an almost infinite variety of valid combinations are possible.

New compounds continue to emerge from our chemical and metallurgical laboratories almost on a daily basis. But it's the knowledge of deep structure that separates the study of chemistry today from the study of alchemy in the past.

You could also liken deep structure to the relatively small set of phonemes from which all human speech and language is constructed. Root

TAPPING INTO THE FOUNDATIONAL STRUCTURE OF KNOWLEDGE

sounds, when combined in ways that are syntactically and semantically correct, make sense. Other combinations which violate the rules of syntax and grammar make no sense. Unless of course, the combination represents a new type of expression, in which case the rules of grammar are modified.

In the knowledge sciences, we refer to this type of system as a *second-order cybernetic system*. It simply means that unlike a first order system in which the rules are "hard-wired" (such as a simple thermostat or the tax tables in an accounting system), a second order cybernetic system can self-modify its rules as conditions change. In more advanced systems, the underlying rules can be modified even in anticipation of changes which may occur in the future.

Sadly, this knowledge of deep structure and its accompanying rules of association have slowly been forgotten as we've amassed our vast human library known as the internet.

Here's one more twist to keep in mind. In deep structure, things don't always line up according to a nice organized set of rules. There are nonlinear structures, including multiple quantum states that a single particle can exhibit at the same instant. These occur because deep structure is stratified.

Two or more discrete states can be present at the same time.

For now you don't need to worry much about such properties other than the fact that they exist. Like geology, you know the earth has tectonic plates moving at extremely slow speeds deep beneath the surface. You don't have to actually see them.

But when those plates suddenly slip, causing an earthquake or even a tsunami, you are reminded of their presence. So it is with human memory.

TAPPING INTO THE FOUNDATIONAL STRUCTURE OF KNOWLEDGE

37

We know engrams exist. And through experiments in neuropsychology and neurophysiology, we know that over time those engrams can become "hard-wired." Sometimes correct associations are made, sometimes erroneous ones. We're progressively learning more about how those associations get programmed in the first place, and how to re-program them if necessary.

This is what deep learning is all about. If somewhere along the line you've been unconsciously programmed into having a fear of or disdain for mathematics or any other subject, that fear or disdain can be replaced with curiosity and enthusiasm. But only through certain types of actions.

That's why we're so adamant about mentally enumerating your observations about a particular topic. The same goes for expressing those observations in handwritten narrative, using #2 pencil on a blank sheet of paper. Those connections to deep memory are vastly different from what you get when banging away at a keyboard or passively listening to an hour-long lecture.

We're not saying you should completely do away with keyboards, displays or even classrooms. They all have their place, as do video games and virtual reality simulations. Just don't let them be your only learning modalities.

As you've seen, there's a forgotten world of deep structure that's been used for centuries by all the great thinkers, scientists and philosophers. Clearly something extraordinary was going on.

We not only need to keep those practices alive, we need to keep uncovering their secrets.

TAPPING INTO THE FOUNDATIONAL STRUCTURE OF KNOWLEDGE

38

Here's an amazing truth you've probably never been taught...

Someone could burn all the books in the world. Erase all the computer memory. Destroy every record.

If that were to happen, the knowledge of mathematics and everything else would still be there, waiting to be re-discovered. Along with all the knowledge that had not yet been discovered in the first place.

That's because knowledge can never be destroyed. Let that sink in. Knowledge cannot be destroyed.

That goes for whatever knowledge you discover yourself. No one can take it from you. It'll always be there.

And if you probe deeply enough, you'll keep making new discoveries. Along with totally unexpected ways for putting those discoveries to use.

There is no other resource on earth that grows the more it's used. Human knowledge literally is the gift that keeps on giving.

DEEP LEARNING MANUAL

Your roadmap to self-discovery

39

Let's recap the steps in the deep learning process. It's important that they become automatic as you continue your knowledge exploration journey. Before long, you'll find yourself applying deep learning not only to your education (lifelong learning), but to your work and everyday life as well.

Deep learning consists of six steps: *thinking; observing; enumerating; expressing; assessing; adjusting.*

1. **Think** of an idea. Anything.
2. **Observe** and experience it directly if you can, or through a book, video, computer simulation, or demonstrated by an instructor or coach. If there's no other way, then picture it in your mind. Not only visually, but using all of your feelings, senses, imagination, and emotions. Like Einstein imagining himself riding on a beam of light.
3. Mentally **enumerate** what you've observed, in short, 30- to 60-second intervals. Make each enumeration totally different from the others.
4. **Express** in your own handwriting what you've observed and experienced. Read what you've written. Refine and adjust. Repeat.

YOUR ROADMAP TO SELF-DISCOVERY

Keep building and growing your personal body of knowledge. Create, design and organize a knowledge space to connect your topics, ideas, and supporting narrative. Organize it visually so you can easily navigate and expand it. Share it with others.

5. **Assess** your progress by periodically stepping back and reviewing what you've written. Develop and apply your personalized version of the four-part assessment rubric of skill, synthesis, evaluativeness and completeness.

   Let your handwritten notes be your teacher. They'll give you insights into how deeply you're learning a particular topic. They'll also help you identify what learning behaviors, positive and negative, are in play.

6. Based on your assessment, think about how you can **adjust** your deep learning approach. It could be sharpening your powers of observation. Or awakening the child in you that always used to ask, "Why? Why? Why?" Or taking steps to overcome your fear of or disdain for something that's been holding you back.

   Use your knowledge space to visually track what topics are known and how well, what topics aren't known, and what topics need further exploration.

And don't forget that extra bonus step, which is…

Repeat. Always be learning. Never quit.

YOUR ROADMAP TO SELF-DISCOVERY

40

Make this six-step process a permanent part of your everyday activity. Keep your journal always at the ready.

It's a lifelong journey, so don't try to change everything at once. Keep making those journal entries. You'll have the satisfaction of seeing the remarkable progress you'll be making over time.

Use this process in school. In your job. As a mentor to guide others. As a lone explorer with an insatiable desire to learn more.

You'll find yourself becoming increasingly more excited and motivated to develop and expand your personal areas of expertise. You'll identify, assess and track those topics about which you need to be most informed. Such as health and nutrition. Personal finance. Politics. Science and the arts.

Best of all, these techniques will help you sift through all the noise. Much of that noise is intended to confuse you, and to position people with the loudest megaphones to come out on top.

Don't be among the millions who say they're drowning in information and starved for knowledge. Be more than informed. Be knowledgeable, which means having the capacity to determine and take the best course of action in any situation.

You'll be confident that your actions will be based not only on what's being presented, but more importantly, on what's hidden deep beneath the surface.

The laboratory that Einstein used for many of his greatest discoveries is still available today, practically for free. Why not grab that same pencil and paper and get started?

Find yourself. Then find your beam of light, and ride it.

Advanced exercises: Expanding your knowledge horizons

Important: you should not attempt these exercises until you've mastered the six steps summarized in Chapter 39.

Those six steps alone will dramatically improve your outlook on learning, as well as your ability to tackle subjects at a level you might never would have attempted otherwise. But it takes time, patience, and persistence.

If you feel you've internalized those steps to the point at which they're becoming habitual and you're still hungry for more, then these remaining chapters will help you grow even further…

ADVANCED EXERCISES: EXPANDING YOUR
KNOWLEDGE HORIZONS

41

Much of mathematics is built upon *set theory*. This includes a branch known as *group theory*.

The threefold structure we discussed earlier (subject, process, object), is a type of group. Specifically, a *dihedral group of order six*. This means there are six and only six ways these three elements can be ordered:

1) Subject → Process → Object
2) Subject → Object → Process
3) Object → Process → Subject
4) Object → Subject → Process
5) Process → Subject → Object
6) Process → Object → Subject

Let's take a closer look at each.

(Subject → Process → Object):

This perspective is essentially "home base," the familiar ordering of subject-verb-object that you learned in grammar school. This represents your view of the world, through your eyes and other senses, along with your beliefs and biases.

(Subject → Object → Process):

From this shift in perspective, you the subject remain the observer, thinking about what the world would look like if process and object switched places. In other words, how you, the observer, would view the process (the new object of observation) through the lens of the object (the new process).

Because these first two transformations view the world through the observer's perspective, we call them the *ego* transformations.

(Object → Process → Subject):

In this transformation, you the subject, and the object (person or thing) with which you are interacting, switch places. This is the first of two *empathy* transformations. This is how a highly empathic individual tends to view the world, through the eyes of others.

(Object → Subject → Process):

This second empathy transformation is a double transformation in which the subject becomes the process, the process becomes the object, and the object becomes the subject. Here the empathic person tries to understand what the person they are trying to help (or thing they are trying to improve) is going through.

ADVANCED EXERCISES: EXPANDING YOUR KNOWLEDGE HORIZONS

What's their situation? What's their environment like? How can it be changed for the better? You'll hear this type of person talking about "walking a mile" in someone else's shoes.

The final two orderings are process transformations.

(Process → Subject → Object):

Here, the observer and process switch places.

(Process → Object → Subject):

This is another double transformation, in which the process becomes the subject, the subject becomes the object, and the object becomes the process.

Trial lawyers tend to master these last two types. For example, a lawyer representing the plaintiff will closely examine what the situation looks like (including pros and cons) when the legal process is viewed from the perspective of the plaintiff (Process → Subject → Object). That same attorney will do the same from the standpoint of the defendant (Process → Object → Subject), looking for strengths and weakness that can either be exploited or that should be avoided.

This is usually what's going on when you see court cases endlessly bogged down in procedural matters. Politics tends to work the same way.

ADVANCED EXERCISES: EXPANDING YOUR KNOWLEDGE HORIZONS

42

In summary, people who are autocratic try to impose their will on both the process and the object. For example, many Apple insiders recall that Steve Jobs was so intense in this regard they referred to him as viewing the world through what they called a "reality distortion field." Being grounded in these two perspectives, he not only transformed entire industries like computers, phones, and music (Subject → Process → Object), he also transformed the engineering and design processes that went into producing those products (Subject → Object → Process).

Empathic individuals try to see the world through the eyes of others, seeking total harmony with everyone (Object → Process → Subject). They see themselves as an instrument for world change and improving people's lives (Object → Subject → Process).

Finally, those who are process-oriented put most of their focus into "winning the case" (Process → Subject → Object). They seem to have an explanation for everything, and tend to get frustrated when they can't find one (Process → Object → Subject).

Here's why these six transformations are so important…

Depending upon your personal profile, you tend to view the world from only one or two perspectives. If that's the case, then you're missing out on four or more different ways of looking at things, along with the added insights, innovations and breakthroughs that come from a more expanded view. Countless critical decisions may be impacted.

Now think of what could happen if you expanded your awareness in such a way that you could view the world from all six perspectives. The same goes for your workgroup. Your family. Legislative bodies. Nations. The world.

ADVANCED EXERCISES: EXPANDING YOUR KNOWLEDGE HORIZONS

43

By practicing these advanced exercises, you are developing the ability to view the world from all six possible perspectives. A few of them will come naturally. Even unconsciously. The rest will require additional effort and attention. This means that from now on, you'll be doing your descriptive enumeration exercises in two parts.

The first part remains the same. You'll come up with a set of orthogonal descriptions of an object of observation. These are from various angles, based on whatever pops into your head.

The new twist is that after you've finished, you'll do a mental check to see from which of the six perspectives you've been making most of your observations.

You may notice that a preponderance of your enumerations come from a process perspective. Or they could be based primarily on empathy. Or ego. And we don't mean ego in a negative sense.

Now go a step further and determine exactly which of the six perspectives you've used. For example, if you're a process person, were your viewpoints based on the perspective of (Process → Subject → Object), (Process → Object →

Subject), or both? This alone will give you valuable insights regarding the lenses through which you tend to view the world.

Now resume the descriptive enumeration exercise from as many of the remaining perspectives as you can. Ultimately aim for drawing from all six.

If you find you can't shift through all of the perspectives without putting some things into writing, then go ahead and capture those thoughts. But use only short notes or mental triggers that you can draw from later when you write the full narrative.

In time, you'll be able to do this more or less habitually.

Let's give it a try…

ADVANCED EXERCISES: EXPANDING YOUR KNOWLEDGE HORIZONS

Action to take:

Go back to your journal and review the narrative you used to express your descriptive enumeration exercise on learning (see Chapters 19-20). Think about which of the six perspectives were in play.

Make a list of the ones that were missing. Now think of how learning looks from the standpoint of each of those missing perspectives.

Close your eyes and make each transformation in your mind, mentally capturing what you've observed. Now express, in handwritten form, any additional insights you've gained as a result of this expanded view.

44

Let's get a little more specific and perform a descriptive enumeration of everyone's favorite subject: *mathematics*. In the threefold structure of knowledge, you are the subject, learning is the process, and mathematics is the object. A simple way to represent the starting point (Subject → Process → Object) is:

You → learn → mathematics

In other words, from the (Subject → Process → Object) perspective, think about what "you learning mathematics" looks like. Feels like. Smells like. Any way you want to describe it.

Now descriptively enumerate the topic of mathematics from the remaining five perspectives. The following are just guidelines; feel free to use your own interpretation:

(Subject → Object → Process): how you impact the process of learning mathematics (for example, your participation in the classroom or online); how venting your joy or frustration spreads negative or positive energy to those around you.

(Object → Process → Subject): what the subject of mathematics does to you; how mathematics changes the way you look at yourself.

ADVANCED EXERCISES: EXPANDING YOUR KNOWLEDGE HORIZONS

(Object → Subject → Process): what mathematics does to your learning process; how mathematics impacts the way you think, feel, observe, and act.

(Process → Subject → Object): what learning does to mathematics; mathematics as seen through the lens of the learning process.

(Process → Object → Subject): What learning mathematics does to you; how learning helps you develop your own brand of math.

You can see how this begins to reveal learning behaviors. For example, you might identify blocking or detrimental traits that have led to and/or reinforced feelings of disdain for mathematics. At the same time, shifting perspectives can open up different pathways to how you approach the subject of mathematics.

Action to take:

Try these six perspectives on any subject, whether it's your favorite, your most dreaded, and everything in between. Going to the dentist, perhaps. Or something like diet and exercise, which many people tend to associate with pain and discomfort. A shift in perspective, such as focusing on health and nutrition, can change something that's perceived as a painful regimen into something pleasant and rewarding.

Afterword

You might be wondering, "Where are the examples?"

We certainly have any number of examples we could have used in this manual. But after long, careful thought, we realized that we'd be contradicting everything we've talked about. We'd be violating our own principles of self-inquiry and self-discovery.

Learning at the surface level consists in large part of "learning by example." There's certainly nothing wrong with that. It's how much of our learning takes place.

But the notion of *tabula rasa* is more powerful than you might realize. A new breakthrough or a clever new way of doing something might be hiding deep inside, just waiting to pop out.

It's easy to go online and dig up a template somebody else put together. After all, why "re-invent the wheel?"

The answer is: "Why *not* re-invent it?" Better yet, try re-framing the question. Think discovery, rather than invention or re-invention. Think not only about the wheel, but the car as well. The whole notion of transportation.

So forget the examples. Stare into space, just like your teacher or boss told you not to do. Be like Steve Jobs, Edwin Land, and countless others who dared to dream. They saw exactly what they wanted to create, just by staring at a blank sheet of paper or an empty table top.

Here's one final thought...

One of the most profound discoveries you'll ever make is that of your own unique signature. Not just how you sign your name, but the complete you. Everything about you. You as the object of observation, as viewed by yourself and others.

Once you do that, you'll present yourself in a way that's totally different from the standard one-size-fits-all label society has been trying to pin on you.

This hidden signature, now coming out into the light, will be your new frame of reference. Your new way of seeing the universe. Completely, as subject, process, and object.

To be expressed on a blank canvas. Ready for you and the world to look at and say, "Wow!"

And don't forget to rinse and repeat.

DEEP LEARNING MANUAL

Appendix: Resources for diving more deeply into deep learning

This book provides only a glimpse into the vast body of knowledge of the field of deep learning, drawing from many decades of research in the knowledge sciences.

Here are just a few of the topics on which our work is based, along with a small sampling of introductory references to get you started, should you want to explore further.

Capturing and expressing knowledge

Trying to express your knowledge about a particular topic can be a daunting challenge. Are you providing too little detail, or too much?

Dr. John Lewis gives you lots of ways to think about codifying knowledge in his book:

The Explanation Age (3rd edition), 2013.

It contains numerous templates and examples, plus a model he calls the "innate lesson cycle." This resource will help guide you through the various phases of discovery, ranging from disrupting the status quo to ideation, design, and implementing change. He also provides ways to capture and express for future reference the thinking behind an idea, including options that were considered along the way, which is rarely done in practice.

Creative sketching

Either as an alternative to or in addition to writing out your thoughts and insights by hand, you should consider sketching and drawing as a means of expression. One of our favorite sources in this regard is Errol Hugh, who never goes anywhere without his sketchbook. A central theme of his work is, *"Life is made of Time; having the mental space to reflect."*

While taking a sabbatical from his practice as a world-renowned architect, he authored two books which contain hundreds of sketches he made during his travels around the world, and the stories and reflections behind them:

The Act of Creative Sketching, published by mmcmcreations, 2012

A Personal Journey Through Sketching: The Sketcher's Art, published by Proverse, Hong Kong, 2009

You can check out his blog at:

sketchingjourney.com

Group theory and the Six Perspectives

Tom McCabe's legendary work in cyclomatic complexity in software has led to even more impactful explorations into human consciousness. As founder of the Expanded Consciousness Institute, he developed the McCabe Prism^{TM}, a tool for looking at problems and solutions through the six lenses of the Dihedral Group of Order Six. His work forms the basis for the advanced exercises at the end of this book. See:

www.expanded-consciousness.com

Knowledge and the Knowledge Sciences

Drs. Alex and David Bennet are the co-founders of the Mountain Quest Institute, which has amassed a treasure trove of research in the knowledge sciences. They've provided invaluable help in reviewing and editing this manual.

While there are many definitions of knowledge, we prefer theirs, which is: *"the capacity (potential or actual) to take effective action in varied and uncertain situations."* You can dive as deeply as you want by reading their book, co-authored with Dr. Joyce Avedisian:

The Course of Knowledge, MQIPress, 2015,

or their latest release, co-authored with Robert Turner:

APPENDIX: RESOURCES FOR DIVING MORE
DEEPLY INTO DEEP LEARNING

<u>Expanding the Self: the Intelligent Complex Adaptive Learning System, a New Theory of Adult Learning</u>, MQIPress, 2015.

Knowledge spaces and learning spaces

For a comprehensive (and very deep) reference on knowledge spaces and learning spaces, along with learning assessments, we recommend the book:

<u>Knowledge Spaces: Applications in Education</u>, by Jean-Claude Falmagne, et al., eds., Springer, 2013.

A shorter version is provided in the paper:

www.aleks.com/about_aleks/Science_Behind_ALEKS.pdf

Two visual tools we use to build knowledge spaces are:

TheBrain:

www.thebrain.com

and

MindManager:

www.mindjet.com/mindmanager

These are commercial products you can purchase at reasonably low cost. If you're among the more tech savvy, you might try a free, open source tool such as C-Map:

www.cmap.ihmc.us

If you're looking to start with something more textual, the wiki has evolved into a useful tool for building a body of knowledge around a collection of topics. It also makes it easy for members of the community to enter, review, validate, and track updates.

Two wikis that we've used are PBworks:

pbworks.com

and the open source Tiki Wiki:

tiki.org

Finally, there's the ever-popular, all-purpose blog. If you choose this route, make sure your blog platform includes tagging, and in particular, the ability to generate and navigate a tag cloud, which is a great way to visually represent the topics in your knowledge space. We use WordPress:

wordpress.com and wordpress.org

APPENDIX: RESOURCES FOR DIVING MORE
DEEPLY INTO DEEP LEARNING

Learning environments

One of our favorite thought leaders in this large and growing area of research is David Thornburg, who uses the campfire, watering hole, cave, and life as metaphors for learning environments:

From the Campfire to the Holodeck: Creating Engaging and Powerful 21st Century Learning Environments, Jossey-Bass, 2014.

We're also influenced by the work of our colleague Dr. Dan Holtshouse, whose Workplace of the Future framework looks at four types of environments for living, working and learning: 1) physical space; 2) information space; 3) organizational space; 4) cognitive space. See:

www.kmworld.com/Articles/Column/The-Future-of-the-Future/The-Future-of-the-Future-The-future-workplace-15811.aspx

also

"Knowledge Work 2020: thinking ahead about knowledge work," On the Horizon, Vol 18, Number 3, 2010

Neuroscience of Deep Learning

Like many areas of research, scientists differ widely in their views on how to model the brain and its functions. Much of our work is based on the late Karl Pribram, whose holonomic model posited a stratified structure in which stable memory elements are formed at the level of conscious awareness (surface learning), while base elements of memory (engrams) occur at a deep level, separated by an epistemic gap:

The Deep and Surface Structure of Memory and Conscious Learning: Toward a 21st Century Model, Brain Center, Radford University, February 20, 1996

and

Non-locality and Localization: A Holographic Hypothesis About Brain Functioning in the Processes of Perception and Memory, Syrlergetics and Psychology, Issue 1: Methodological Issues, Moscow, MGSU Union, 1997, pp. 156-183 (in Russian).

and

Brain and Perception: Holonomy and Structure in Figural Processing, Lawrence Erlbaum Associates, 1991.

APPENDIX: RESOURCES FOR DIVING MORE
DEEPLY INTO DEEP LEARNING

Many of Pribram's 700 published papers can be found at:

www.karlpribram.com/data-papers/

Dr. Paul S. Prueitt worked with Pribram and formulated a theory of learning patterned after observations of immune system behaviors, whereby repeated activity at the surface level of conscious awareness induces an acquired learning disability that inhibits deep learning:

Continuous Analogs to Discrete Dynamical Systems with Application to Modeling Biological Response, Hampton University, 1989.

also:

Individually Directed Inquiry: Foundational Concepts and Challenges, R. L. Moore Legacy Conference, 2014.

Self-directed inquiry and self-directed learning

Self-directed inquiry was the preferred approach to education prior to the nineteenth century. An insightful look into its practice during the enlightenment and how it influenced the American founders can be found in the paper:

Huey B. Long and M. L. Ashford, *Self-Directed Inquiry as a Method of Education in Colonial America*, The Journal of General Education, The Pennsylvania State University Press, Vol. 28, No. 3 (Fall 1976).

See also, the International Journal of Self-Directed Learning, and the International Society for Self-Directed Learning (ISSDL):

www.sdlglobal.com

Index

anxiety (about a topic or subject), 92
assessment, 62, 64–75, 78, 93, 96, 97, 119, 145
bias, 90, 93, 125
blank paper test, 6, 48, 56, 68, 72
Branson, Sir Richard, 51
categories, 54–57, 69, 72, 73
Catholic Church, 107, 108
CERN, 108
completeness, 21, 26, 32, 66
complexity, 6, 26, 29, 68, 92, 95, 143, 145
conceptual graph, 54
confidence, 6, 16, 68, 92, 95
deep structure, vi, 38, 104, 110–12, 114
descriptive enumeration, 20–27, 32, 34, 38, 40, 45, 56, 59, 61, 64, 72, 94–98, 118, 131–34
dihedral group, 125, 144
disdain (for a topic or subject), 97, 99, 113, 119, 135
Douglass, Frederick, 42
dyslexia, 51, 78, 83
Edison, Thomas, 42
education, 7, 72, 74, 83, 100, 118, 149
Einstein, Albert, 4, 15, 64, 118, 122
emotion, 16, 24, 26, 83, 91, 92, 118
entanglement (quantum), 107
evaluativeness, 66, 68, 71, 73, 78, 119
fear, 26, 41, 47–50, 72, 92, 95, 113, 119
Franklin, Benjamin, 42
Galileo, 107, 108
group theory, 125, 143
handwriting, 11, 40, 48, 50, 90, 91, 95, 96, 118
handwritten notes, vi, 38–46, 54, 56, 64, 72, 90–96, 107, 113, 119, 133
Hitler, Adolph, 42
Hubble Space Telescope, 108
imagination, 13–16, 64, 86, 118
industrial revolution, 42
information age, iii, 42
intuition, 16
Jobs, Steve, 34, 129, 138

journal, 10–13, 17, 20, 45, 59–64, 91, 121, 133
knowledge
  body of, iv, 54, 57, 64, 119, 141, 146
  deep knowledge, 62, 67, 104
  definition, 144
  knowledge sciences, iv, 111, 141, 144
  knowledge space, 54–58, 73–75, 83, 87, 96, 98, 119, 145, 146
  threefold structure, 105–10, 125, 134
Land, Edwin, 138
learning
  acquired learning disabilities, vii, 51, 78, 149
  behaviors, vi, 32, 62, 65, 68, 78–94, 119, 135
  deep learning, vii, 2, 4, 6, 11, 26, 47, 51, 54, 60–69, 74, 84, 90, 95, 104, 105, 113, 118, 119, 141
  disabilities, 78, 83
  environment, 86, 147
  learning space, 58, 74, 87, 96, 145
  lifelong, 74, 118, 121
  objectives, 73
  rote, vi, vii, 4, 28–31
  surface-level or "shallow", 2, 4, 29, 42, 51, 64, 67, 78, 83, 86, 90, 137, 148, 149
Library of Congress Card Catalog, 56
Lincoln, Abraham, 42
Madonna, 45
mathematics, vii, 26, 47, 48, 95, 97–101, 104, 113, 115, 125, 134, 135
memory, 21, 24, 28, 38, 104, 112–15, 148
  engrams, vi, 104, 110, 148
mind map, 54, 55
neurophysiology, 113
neuropsychology, 113
Newton, Isaac, 39, 64
observation, 16, 20, 24, 28, 39, 41, 98, 106, 110, 113, 131
  object of, 21–25, 38, 54, 59, 64, 98, 106–9, 126, 131, 138
  powers of, 20, 32, 119
orthogonality, 26, 32, 38, 64, 131
passion, 95–100
questions, 6, 29, 68, 79, 87, 92, 93, 99, 137

INDEX

reflexivity, 39, 107
Rorschach test, 22
scatter and gather, 72
Sculley, John, 34
second-order cybernetic system, 111
self-awareness, 84, 130
self-discovery, iii, v, vi, vii, 2, 5, 33, 34, 47, 68, 137, 138
self-image, 93
set theory, 125
Shakespeare, Willam, 39
Simpson, Bart, 84
skill, 66, 67, 70, 73, 78, 119

STEM (Science, Technology, Engineering and Mathematics), 100
synthesis, 66–71, 73, 78, 119
tabula rasa, 10, 35, 38, 137
technology, iii, 4, 21
time-invariant, 105, 108, 110
topics, 38, 39, 50, 54–57, 73–75, 87, 97, 118–21, 141, 146
writing to learn, 13

About the author

For over thirty years, Dr. Art Murray and his teams have helped individuals and organizations capture, share, and grow their deeply embedded knowledge. His clients include government agencies, non-profit organizations, and companies of all sizes cross the globe.

He is CEO of Applied Knowledge Sciences, Inc., and Chief Technology Officer of the Second School Network. He holds a B.S.E.E. from Lehigh University, and the M.E.A. and D.Sc. degrees from The George Washington University. His column "The Future of the Future" appears in KMWorld Magazine.